CONTENTS

INTRODUCTION

Section 282 of the *Catechism of the Catholic Church* (hereafter *CCC*) assures us that knowing what happens at the end of human history is "decisive for the meaning and orientation of our life and actions." Our view of the end times determines our view of salvation history. Knowing what happens at the end of our lives and at the end of human history is of supreme importance for understanding why God made us and what He has planned for us both in this life and in the next.

Unfortunately, many non-Catholic groups today are promoting serious errors about the last things. Sadly, many Catholics are vulnerable in this area because they don't know the Church's teaching about the end times.

In this booklet we give the basic teachings of the Catholic Church on the end times, and we deal with some of the more common errors.

A correct understanding of the last things helps us live this life with great peace and hope. It also gives us a deeper appreciation of how much God loves us and how great a gift we have in being made in His image. Unlike some pagan religions that believe human history repeats itself endlessly with no ultimate purpose, we Christians believe that human history in this world is moving toward a climactic finale. This end will fully reveal the meaning of human history.

THE SECOND COMING

Virtually all Christians agree with Catholics that Jesus Christ will one day return and put an end to this world as we know it. Beyond this core belief, however, we find serious diversions from Catholic teachings about Christ's Second Coming. Among the many reasons for these errors, at least two are due to historical oversights:

① Failure to understand that many prophecies in the book of Daniel were fulfilled in the time of the Maccabees. Since Protestant Bibles leave out 1 and 2 Maccabees, this oversight is understandable.

② Lack of familiarity with the events surrounding the destruction of the Jewish Temple in AD 70.

We will identify other reasons as we deal with the various aspects of the Second Coming.

WHAT SIGNS WILL PRECEDE THE SECOND COMING?

Chapter 24 of Matthew gives many of the signs that will precede the Second Coming. We have to read these signs carefully because some were to occur before the destruction of the Temple in AD 70. Others refer to the Second Coming at the end of time. To make matters more difficult, some of the signs could relate to *both* events.

Thus, identifying exactly which signs refer to which events in Matthew 24 is not easy. Happily, several New Testament (NT) letters and the book of Revelation identify several events clearly linked to the Second Coming. We will examine these first, and then deal with Matthew 24.

➤ **The thousand-year reign**, also known as the Millennium (Revelation 20). Although the Catholic Church has not officially defined the Millennium, the common view, following St. Augustine,[1] is that the number 1000 is figurative and represents the time *between* the first and second coming of Christ. In this interim before His Second Coming, Jesus is reigning through His Church and the power of Satan is diminished. Satan will be allowed greater power closer to the Second Coming. This will bring a severe trial for the Church (Revelation 20:7–9, *CCC* 675). We will discuss the Dispensationalist view of the Millennium in the section on the Rapture.

> **Revelation 20:1–8:** [An angel] seized the dragon, that ancient serpent, who is the Devil and Satan, and bound him for a thousand years.... [Martyrs] came to life, and reigned with Christ a thousand years.... And when the thousand years are ended, Satan will be loosed from his prison and will come out to deceive the nations....

---

1 *City of God*, book XX, especially chapters 7–9.

➢ **The rise of the Antichrist** (1 John 2:18–23, 2 Thessalonians 2:3–4, Revelation 13, *CCC* 675–676). The Antichrist, called by St. Paul "the man of lawlessness" and "the beast" in Revelation 13, will be the ultimate false prophet. He will launch a fearful persecution of the Church (*CCC* 675) even as he seduces the masses with lying wonders (2 Thessalonians 2:9–10).

> **1 John 2:18:** as you have heard that anti-christ is coming, so now many antichrists have come....

> **2 Thessalonians 2:3–10:** Let no one deceive you in any way; for that day will not come, unless the rebellion comes first, and the man of lawlessness is revealed.... The coming of the lawless one by the activity of Satan will be with all power and with pretended signs and wonders, and with all wicked deception....

➢ **A mass apostasy** (2 Thessalonians 2:3, Revelation 13:3, Matthew 24:11–12, and Luke 18:8). The Bible teaches that before the Second Coming there will be a massive falling away from the Christian faith. Many people will be deceived by false prophets, especially the ultimate false prophet, the Antichrist.

➢ **The conversion of the Jews** (Romans 11). Before the Second Coming, the Jews will accept Jesus as the Messiah.

> **Romans 11:25–26:** I want you to understand this mystery, brethren: a hardening has come upon part of Israel, until the full number of the Gentiles come in, and so all Israel will be saved....

➢ **The preaching of the Gospel to the whole world** (Matthew 24:14). This undoubtedly means more than simply broadcasting the Gospel through the media and the internet. It will be an evangelization that will implant the Gospel in every nation and greatly diminish the influence of non-Christian religions.

> **Matthew 24:14:** And this gospel of the kingdom will be preached throughout the whole world ... and then the end will come.

➢ **The appearance of the sign of Christ in the sky** (Matthew 24:30). This is generally believed to refer to a cross.

> **Matthew 24:30:** then will appear the sign of the Son of man in heaven, and then all the tribes of the earth will mourn, and they will see the Son of man coming on the clouds of heaven....

➢ **Frightening signs in the sky; severe natural and man-made calamities** (Matthew 24, Luke 21:25–26). Some of these occurred at the destruction of the Jewish Temple in AD 70. We should assume that even those signs related to the temple's destruction will have multiple fulfillments and will occur to a greater extent before the Second Coming. Beginning with Adam and Eve, we see that upheavals in nature accompany an increase in evil. Nature became disordered after the rebellion of our first parents. Later, history repeatedly records severe natural calamities in times of widespread wickedness. We should therefore expect that, in the time of supreme evil before the Second Coming, natural calamities will peak. That *man-made* calamities increase in times of extreme evil is self-evident.

> **Matthew 24:29:** Immediately after the tribulation of those days the sun will be darkened, and the moon will not give its light, and the stars will fall from heaven, and the powers of the heavens will be shaken....

> **Luke 21:25:** And there will be signs in sun and moon and stars, and upon the earth distress of nations in perplexity at the roaring of the sea and the wave....

WHY WERE WE GIVEN THE SIGNS OF THE SECOND COMING?

Christ flatly states that not one can know the date of the Second Coming (Matthew 24:42). So the signs are obviously not for calculating the day of His return. Moreover, we can't use the signs to determine the date for the following reasons:

① The exact sequences are not given.

② The time intervals are not given.

③ Many of the signs obviously have multiple fulfillments; we cannot know if a greater fulfillment is yet to come.

We *were* given the signs of the Second Coming for the following reasons:

① To remind us how fragile this life is and how vulnerable we are to evil assault.

② To remind us that, even if we don't live to see the Second Coming, we will each still experience the end of our world at death.

③ To help us understand the nature of the spiritual conflict that surrounds us, and the need for vigilance and discernment.

④ To remind us that, while the devils are formidable enemies, God's power is immeasurably greater.

CAN WE KNOW THE DATE OF THE SECOND COMING?

Our Lord teaches that the date of His return *cannot* be known in advance. In Matthew 24:42, Jesus assures us, "you do not know on what day your Lord is coming." In Matthew 24:43, He compares His return to the coming of a thief to emphasize in the strongest terms that His arrival cannot be foreknown.[2]

Despite the clear teachings of Our Lord, there have always been those who insisted they knew when Christ was returning. Even while the Apostles were still alive, people claimed to know that Jesus' coming was at hand (2 Thessalonians 2:2). Thus, it isn't surprising that after the close of the apostolic age, the problem of date setters would continue.

In the latter part of the 2nd century, a man named Montanus, founder of the sect of Montanism, claimed the heavenly Jerusalem was going to descend in his time in the town of Pepuza, in modern day Turkey. This

---

2 See also: Matthew 25:13, Luke 17:22–35, 1 Thessalonians 5:2, and 2 Peter 3:10.

heretical sect was compelling enough to seduce Tertullian, one of the early Church's brightest theologians.

This should be a lesson to us: date setters can be very convincing in their interpretations of Sacred Scripture. We must be anchored by the Church's teachings and a spirit of discernment.

Not surprisingly, when the end of the first millennium approached, many people were convinced the end of the world was near. Again, when the Black Plague devastated Europe in the 14th century, many were convinced the end was upon them.

In the 19th century, the United States saw an explosion of groups promoting the Second Coming (also known as Adventism). As we would expect, that century had a large number of date setters. The founders of the Mormons, Jehovah's Witnesses, and Seventh Day Adventists each predicted the date of Christ's return. Each date came and went; nothing happened.

Some of the date setters cleverly misuse Sacred Scripture. In the 1980s, one evangelist maintained that while Christ clearly told us that we could not know the *day* or *hour* of His return, we *could* nevertheless know the *year*! He then made a compelling argument for the year 1993. He wrenched Jesus' teachings totally out of context. He also ignored passages like Acts 1:7 that tell us we cannot know the times or seasons: "[Jesus] said to them, 'It is *not for you to know times or seasons* which the Father has fixed by his own authority.'" The Catholic Church plainly affirms that we cannot know the date of Christ's return (*CCC* 673). "Only the Father knows the day and the hour; only he determines the moment of its coming" (*CCC* 1040).

Our Lord chose not to reveal the time of His return for good reasons. He knows human nature. He knows we tend to procrastinate. God put us in this world to gain the glory He has called us to, and to convert the world to Christ. What would happen if people knew when the world would end?

We can answer that question by asking: how would people live if they knew when they were going to die? Strong Christians would strive to gain as much glory as possible. But many people would grow slack and wait until right before death to get serious about their faith. For example, college students often delay their term papers for weeks on end. Then, the day before it's due, they work all night only to turn in a shoddy product. Many people wait until April 14 to start on their income taxes resulting in a mad scramble.

This is human nature. We drag our feet and delay when it comes to tasks we don't want to do. We wind them up at the last minute with poor results. We don't consider that we might get sick right before a deadline and not be able to meet it at all.

Likewise, if at twenty we knew we would live until ninety, we would be strongly tempted to delay the struggles of the spiritual life until we were eighty-nine! We can see how damaging this would be for our souls. Think how much more grace we would gain if we lived those sixty-nine years prepared to die at any time.

We can apply this example to humanity as a whole if we knew when the world would end. Those who knew that the end of the world was *far off* would count on living a normal lifespan. Many would not consider that they might die any moment, and would be tempted to put off their conversion and sanctification. Those who knew the end of the world was *near* would be tempted to give up the work of transforming the world for Christ—why polish the silver on a sinking ship? Strong Christians would work harder for Christ if they knew the end were near, but most people would neglect the needs of the world and focus on preparing their own souls.

Uncertainty about when the world will end, like uncertainty about when our lives will end, is good for us spiritually. It helps us exercise and strengthen the virtues of faith and hope. We become watchful and vigilant. We are driven to gain all the grace we can, for as long as we can.

WHAT IS THE MANNER OF CHRIST'S RETURN?

While Jesus doesn't want us to know the date of His return, He does want us to know the *manner* of His return. This way, we won't be taken in by false Christs or false teachings about Christ's Second Coming.

Throughout history, many false prophets have claimed to be the returned Christ. In the early 1980s, there was widespread interest in a New Age Christ, who was supposed to be revealed at that time. Compelling announcements appeared in major newspapers worldwide. Even some Christians wondered if he might be the returned Jesus. The ads said he was in some room in London. Christians forgot the teaching of Matthew 24:26: "So, if they say to you, 'Lo, he is in the wilderness,' do not go out; if they say, 'Lo, he is in the inner rooms,' do not believe it."

Jehovah's Witnesses' claim Christ returned invisibly in 1914. Fundamentalists teach that Jesus will return secretly to gather up (rapture) the elect. This concept seduces many today. Knowing the manner of the Second Coming protects us from false claims and teachings.

The Bible teaches the following about the manner of Christ's Coming:

① Christ will return *once and once only*. Sacred Scripture teaches only one return of Christ. We will cover this teaching in more detail in the section on the rapture.

② Christ's return will be *public* and *visible*. "Behold, he is coming with the clouds, and *every eye will see him*" (Revelation 1:7). "All the tribes of the earth ... will *see* the Son of man coming on the clouds" (Matthew 24:30). His return will be like *lightning* shining from east to west (Matthew 24:27). He will be announced by a "*loud* trumpet call" (Matthew 24:31). And "all the angels" will accompany Him (Matthew 25:31).

③ Christ will return "coming on the *clouds* of heaven with power and great glory" (Matthew 24:30). "And when he had said this, as they were looking on, he was lifted up, and a cloud took him out of their sight. And while they were gazing into heaven as he went, behold, two men stood by them in white robes, and said, ... 'This Jesus, who was taken up from you into heaven, will come *in the same way* as you saw him go into heaven'" (Acts 1:9–11).

④ Christ's return will bring about the *end of the world* and the *final judgment* (Matthew 25). "When the Son of man comes in his glory, and all the angels with him, then he will sit on his glorious throne. Before him will be gathered all the nations, and he will separate them one from another ... " (Matthew 25:31–32).

As we can see, what the Bible teaches about the manner of Christ's return rules out invisible comings and secret raptures. It also rules out Christ hiding in some room in London or anyplace else.

The cases we cited earlier may appear to be no-brainers for Christians who know their faith. But you can be sure that in the future, seductive false prophets will present phony comings that will test even the elect: "False Christs and false prophets will arise and show signs and wonders, to lead astray, if possible, the elect" (Mark 13:22). Therefore, we must cling to the Bible passages cited above, and pray for a spirit of discernment.

WHAT HAPPENS AT THE SECOND COMING?

① The *end of the world*, as we have already seen.

② The *end of time*. Only eternity remains after the Second Coming.

③ The *end of Purgatory*. The common teaching of the Church is that whoever is left in Purgatory will enter heaven at this time.

④ The *end of death*. Those who are alive at the Second Coming will not experience death (1 Corinthians 15:51; 1 Thessalonians 4:17).

⑤ The *General Resurrection*. The bodies of all the dead will rise (John 5:27–29; 11:23–24). The bodies of the damned will rise to a condition of immortality. They will be reunited to their souls and experience eternal torment. The bodies of the saved will rise not only to immortality but also glory. They will be reunited to their souls and experience eternal bliss.

Those who are alive and not in the state of grace will be changed body and soul into the condition of the damned. Those who are alive and in the state of grace will be changed body and soul into the condition of glory. These changes will not involve death, as we mentioned in ④. The resurrected bodies of the elect will shine like the sun (Matthew 13:43). They will be incapable of suffering, illness, and death, because they will have the quality of incorruptibility (1 Corinthians 15:42). The elects' resurrected bodies will be solid flesh and bones

(Luke 24:39), but they will have spiritual powers (1 Corinthians 15:44) enabling them to travel any distance at the speed of thought and also to pass through solid objects.

⑥ The *General Judgment* (Matthew 25:31–46, Revelation 20:1–15). The entire human race will be gathered for this awesome tribunal that will reveal the entirety of human history. After the General Judgment, no questions about this history will remain. Everything will be made known. God will mete out final judgment and final reward. The devils and their human followers will be cast into hell forever.

After the General Judgment, only heaven and hell remain. Those who died before the Second Coming were judged at the moment of death—in their particular judgment—and already know their eternal destiny. Those who are alive at the Second Coming will have their eternal destiny revealed at the moment Christ returns. The General Judgment is also known as the Last Judgment and the Great White Throne Judgment (Revelation 20:11).

⑦ The *universal restoration* (Acts 3:21, 1 Corinthians 15:28, *CCC* 671, 769). After the General Judgment, the Church will be perfected in glory and reign eternally as the New Jerusalem (Revelation 21). The Church will then consist of perfect saints only (the Church triumphant). The Church on earth (the Church militant) and the Church in Purgatory (the Church suffering) will no longer exist. The material universe will be melted down by fire and recreated by God into the new heavens and the new earth (2 Peter 3:12–13). Just as our weak mortal bodies will be transfigured at the Resurrection to a condition of beauty, majesty, perfection, and glory, so too will the material world, which currently shares our condition of imperfection (Romans 8:19–22), be recreated to a condition of perfection and beauty so it can be part of our life in heaven.

> **2 Peter 3:12–13:** the coming of the day of God, because of which the heavens will be kindled and dissolved, and the elements will melt with fire! But according to his promise we wait for new heavens and a new earth in which righteousness dwells.

THE RAPTURE

Rapture fever is sweeping the land. We hear about it from television and radio evangelists. We read about it in best-selling books. We encounter people everywhere who are talking about the rapture that is coming soon.

Catholics wonder what this is all about. They don't remember being taught about a rapture in their catechism. Yet these Fundamentalists state that the rapture is plainly taught in Sacred Scripture. They point to Bible verses that appear to confirm their belief in the rapture.

Tens of millions of Christians, including many Catholics, have read best-sellers like *The Late Great Planet Earth* and the *Left Behind* series. These books promote a Fundamentalist view of the rapture that is very appealing in many ways. Many Catholics have adopted this belief without realizing how unbiblical and anti-Catholic it is. The gripping tales of the *Left Behind* series are introducing millions to a belief system with serious errors about Christ's Coming and the nature of His Church.

It is vital that Catholics understand this erroneous view of the rapture and be able to refute it. We will first give the Catholic view, and then the Fundamentalist view. Finally, we will show why the Fundamentalist view of the rapture is gravely flawed.

Dispensationalism, including the theory of the "secret rapture" was popularized in the 1909 Schofield Study Bible and the recent Left Behind books.

THE CATHOLIC VIEW

The word "rapture" comes from the Latin word which means "to be caught up" or "taken up." It refers to the passage in 1 Thessalonians 4:17. Catholics believe St. Paul is teaching that those believers who are alive at Christ's Second Coming will not experience death. Rather, they will be gloriously transformed and join (by being caught up or raptured) the saints who are already with Christ. The Catholic interpretation of this passage is also the belief of Orthodox Christians, most Protestants, and even many Fundamentalists.

> **1 Thessalonians 4:17:** then we who are alive, who are left, shall be **caught up** together with them in the clouds to meet the Lord in the air; and so we shall always be with the Lord.

THE FUNDAMENTALIST VIEW

The phrase "Fundamentalist view of the rapture" is misleading, since not all Fundamentalists accept it. However, since many Fundamentalist Protestants promote this view, it has come to be associated with them. Technically, it should be called the *Dispensationalist* view of the rapture. What is this belief and where did it come from?

In the 19th century, this country saw an explosion of

movements and groups focusing on Christ's return (Adventism). One of the Adventist movements was called Dispensationalism. Founded by John Nelson Darby in 1830, Dispensationalism was a bizarre way of interpreting the Bible. It divided salvation history into seven distinct periods, or dispensations, each with its own role and purpose in God's plan. We will focus on two aspects only of this complicated system that relate to the current problems with the rapture:

① its view of *Christ's coming*, and

② its view of the *Church*.

Darby taught that at Christ's first coming, the nation of Israel rejected Him, so He turned to the Gentiles instead. Jesus established the Church to gather together those Gentiles destined for salvation. In the meantime, He temporarily turned away from the Jews to punish them. This caused Israel's "prophetic clock" to stop ticking. All of Israel's Old Testament (OT) prophecies and promises were put on hold.

Dispensationalists view the Church as only a makeshift, temporary solution until Israel returns to the fold.

When the time of the Gentiles is fulfilled (Luke 21:24), Jesus will return in a *secret* coming to take the Church (Gentile believers) to heaven. They will be taken up (raptured) to meet Jesus in the clouds and then return with Him to heaven. The purpose of the Church will be over. Then begins a seven-year period of tribulation and destruction on earth, during which time the Antichrist will reign. After the seven-year tribulation, Jesus will return *publicly* and defeat the Antichrist and his followers.

The Jews will then accept Christ as their Savior and become the kingdom people. Christ will literally reign on earth for a thousand years (the Millennium of Revelation 20:4), ruling over the restored nation of Israel. Israel's prophetic clock will begin ticking again. During this time, all the Old Testament prophecies regarding Israel will be fulfilled. Israel will re-establish the OT religion with its rituals and animal sacrifices. This is the kingdom Jesus talks about in the gospel (Matthew 4:17, 16:19, among others). Israel will be the kingdom people again, since the Jews have always been God's chosen ones. The Church was only a makeshift, temporary solution until Israel returned to the fold. After the thousand years are over, Satan will be unleashed and quickly conquered, and the world will finally come to an end.

This brief overview explains why Fundamentalists who embrace Dispensationalism focus on the nation of Israel, and why they have such a low view of the Church (just a temporary stopgap). This is also why they see the creation of the state of Israel in 1948 as so critical. Dispensationalists believe this event restarted Israel's prophetic clock. They believe the nation of Israel is poised to become the kingdom people once more. Thus the rapture is imminent. The Church, having served its temporary purpose, will soon be caught up (raptured).

12

PROBLEMS WITH THE DISPENSATIONALIST VIEW OF THE RAPTURE

➤ A Faulty View of the Church

The belief that the Church is a makeshift measure for the benefit of the Gentiles is unbiblical. So is the notion that the kingdom Jesus preached is a future restored Israel. In Matthew 4:17 Jesus said, "the kingdom of heaven is *at hand*." In Matthew 16:13–20, when Jesus taught that He will establish His Church on the Rock (St. Peter), He told Peter, "I will give *you* [not someone in the distant future] the keys of the kingdom of heaven."

Sacred Scripture calls the Church the Body of Christ (Ephesians 5:23; Colossians 1:24), the New Jerusalem (Revelation 21:2[3]), the Kingdom of heaven (Matthew 13), the Bride of Christ that Jesus marries at the end of time (Revelation 21:9). Jesus said He would be with His Church all days, until the end of time (Matthew 28:20).

> *The Kingdom of God is the Church.*

The idea that the Church is merely a passing phase until the restored kingdom of Israel arrives is found nowhere in Sacred Scripture. Worse, this view contradicts clear biblical evidence that the Kingdom of God is the *Church*. Leading promoters of this false view of the rapture teach that the Catholic Church is the false religion that will align itself with the Antichrist—the Whore of Babylon (Revelation 18)!

➤ A Faulty View of Israel

The OT is fulfilled in the NT. The OT priesthood is fulfilled in the priesthood of Christ. The OT sacrifices were fulfilled in the sacrifice of Calvary. Likewise, the OT Israel is fulfilled in the NT Church—the New Israel of God (Galatians 6:16). OT prophecies regarding Israel find their ultimate fulfillment in the Church. There will be *no* return to the OT Israel as God's covenant people since the NT Church is the new and eternal covenant people of God.

> *The Church is the new and eternal covenant people of God.*

To equate the current nation of Israel—created in 1948 by the United Nations, a secular, anti-Christian institution—with the OT covenant nation of Israel shows a faulty understanding of both history and Scripture. The OT Israel was established by God on Mount Sinai as part of the OT covenant given to Moses. That is why Israel was a covenant nation. The current nation of Israel has no religious significance to us as Christians. However, we do believe the Jews are still in God's plan, as St. Paul teaches in Romans 11. One day they will enter the Church and become part of the NT chosen people.

---

[3] Compare Revelation 21:14 and Ephesians 2:19–22.

➤ *A Faulty Reading of 1 Thessalonians 4*

Nowhere in 1 Thessalonians 4 does St. Paul teach a secret coming of Christ. In this passage, Paul teaches the resurrection of the dead at Christ's Second Coming. The Thessalonians were apparently concerned that Christians who died before Jesus' Second Coming would not share in His triumphant return. Paul assures the Thessalonians that "the dead in Christ will rise first." Then Christians who are still alive will join the resurrected and "*together with **them**… meet the Lord in the air*." Thus, "we shall always be with the Lord."

> **1 Thessalonians 4:13–17:** But we would not have you ignorant, brethren, *concerning those who are asleep*, that you may not grieve as others do who have no hope. For since we believe that Jesus died and rose again, even so, through Jesus, *God will bring with him those who have fallen asleep*. For this we declare to you by the word of the Lord, that we who are alive, who are left until the <u>coming of the Lord</u>, shall not precede those who have fallen asleep. For the Lord himself will descend from heaven with a <u>cry of command</u>, with the <u>archangel's call</u>, and with the <u>sound of the trumpet</u> of God. And *the dead in Christ will rise first*; then we who are alive, who are left, shall be <u>caught up together</u> *with them* <u>in the clouds</u> to meet the Lord in the air; and *so we shall always be with the Lord*. Therefore comfort one another with these words.

Paul's primary concern is to console the Thessalonians with the truth that *all* Christians will meet Christ at His Second Coming. No one, including the dead, will be left behind. The dead will be raised, the living will join them, and *together* they will share in Christ's triumphant descent from heaven to earth.

St. Paul speaks of Christ's coming, not coming*s*, ruling out more than one. He says that Christ's coming will be announced by the *cry of an archangel* and by a *trumpet blast*: this is no secret rapture. According to Paul, those who will be caught up (raptured) to meet the Lord in the air are those who have survived, meaning those who have survived until the end of the world.

Nowhere does this passage teach that Jesus will secretly come to snatch away Christians from the earth and whisk them back to heaven to escape the seven-year tribulation. There is no mention of seven years or the tribulation.

More importantly, there is no mention of Jesus suddenly switching directions. Notice that Jesus "will descend *from* heaven." He will come from heaven *to* earth. It doesn't say anything about Jesus suddenly making a U-turn after Christians meet Him in the air (see box on page 16). Rather, this passage is describing Christ's triumphant return to earth and the resurrection of the dead that will accompany it.

In 1 Corinthians 15:50–58, St. Paul addresses the same issue of the generation that will not die. But he adds some important details. The trumpet blast is the blast of the *last* trumpet. Death is ended: "Death is swallowed up in victory" (1 Corinthians 15:54). Obviously, St. Paul is speaking about the coming of Christ at the end of the world.

14

> **1 Corinthians 15:51-52:** We shall not all sleep, but we shall all be changed, in a moment, in the twinkling of an eye, <u>at the last trumpet</u>. For the <u>trumpet will sound</u>, and the <u>dead will be raised</u> imperishable, and we shall be changed.

Matthew 24:29–31 describes the *same event* as 1 Thessalonians 4. Both passages include Christ coming in the clouds, angels, the trumpet blast, and the gathering of the elect (see chart on page 15). Yet, most Dispensationalists agree that Matthew 24:29–31 refers to Christ's coming at the end of time.

> **Matthew 24:29–31:** *Immediately after the tribulation* of those days … then will appear the sign of the Son of man in heaven, and then all the tribes of the earth will mourn, and they will see the Son of man <u>coming on the clouds</u> of heaven with power and great glory; and he will send out his <u>angels</u> with <u>a loud trumpet call</u>, and they will <u>gather his elect</u> from the four winds, from one end of heaven to the other.

Since Matthew 24:29–31 describes Christ's coming at the end of time, as rapture proponents agree, and since 1 Thessalonians 4:13–18 describes the *same event*, the rapture occurs *at* Christ's coming at the end of time. The rapture cannot occur *before* the tribulation, but "immediately after the tribulation" at Christ's Second Coming.

2 Thessalonians 2:1,3,8 also confirms that the rapture does not occur *before* the tribulation, but rather *after* the apostasy (the rebellion) and the revelation of the anti-Christ (the man of lawlessness). Thus, the rapture (our assembling to meet Him) does not *precede* a seven-year tribulation and Jesus' Second Coming. Instead, the rapture *coincides* with Christ's Second Coming at the end of time.

> **2 Thessalonians 2:1,3,8:** Now concerning the <u>coming of our Lord Jesus Christ</u> and <u>our assembling to meet him</u>…. Let no one deceive you in any way; for *that day will not come, unless the rebellion comes first, and the man of lawlessness is revealed….* [A]nd the Lord Jesus will slay him with the breath of his mouth and *destroy him by his appearing and his coming.*

The rapture does not occur *before* the tribulation, but *after* the tribulation, the rebellion, and the anti-Christ. The rapture occurs *at* the last trumpet, as Christ comes again at the end of time.

➤ *A Faulty Interpretation of Matthew 24:38–41*

Dispensationalists teach that, in these verses, those taken away are snatched up in the secret rapture. But notice: nothing in this passage speaks of a secret rapture or coming. The context is very clear: Jesus is using these examples to emphasize the suddenness and unexpectedness of His return. These Dispensationalists are reading a secret rapture *into* the text; it certainly does not flow immediately *from* the text.

> **Matthew 24:38–41:** For as in those days before the flood … they did not know until the flood came and swept them all away, so will be the coming of the Son of man. Then two men will be in the field; one is taken and one is left. Two women will be grinding at the mill; one is taken and one is left.

If we look at the parallel passage in Luke 17:22–37, Jesus again uses the example of the flood to emphasize the suddenness of His return. He adds another example, the destruction of Sodom. Both events illustrate the same point: the suddenness of judgment.

There is no teaching of a secret rapture here. Our Lord begins this passage by saying the day of the Son of man will be *obvious*: "as the lightning flashes and lights up the sky from one side to the other" (verse 24). There's nothing secret about lightning. Jesus explicitly says that just as judgment in the time of Noah and Lot occurred without warning, "so will it be on the day when the Son of man is *revealed*" (verse 30). Revealed is the opposite of hidden. This day refers to Christ's public coming and sudden judgment at the end of time. Our Lord's return will be obvious: as obvious as the flood, as obvious as the destruction of Sodom, as obvious as lightning.

Some rapture proponents try to use the events of Noah's flood and the destruction of Lot's Sodom to support their theory that the righteous are raptured while the wicked are left behind on earth. In both cases, however, the ones who were *snatched away* (raptured) were the *wicked*.[4] The ones who *remained on earth* were the *righteous*! This is the very opposite of rapture theory.

➤ *No Record in History*

If the secret rapture of the Church were true, we should expect such a momentous event to be explicitly taught in the Bible and by the early Church Fathers. In fact, Scripture never teaches more than one future coming. The "coming" of Christ is always *singular* and refers to His coming at the end of time. Likewise, the Fathers of the Church always teach *one* future coming at the end of time.

These four passages describe the same event: the Second Coming.
Notice the clear parallels between 1 Thessalonians 4:13–17 and the other passages.

1 Thess 4:13–17	Matt 24:29–31	2 Thess 2:1,3,8	1 Cor 15:51–52
"coming of the Lord"	"Son of man coming"	"coming of our Lord Jesus Christ"	—
"archangel's call"	"angels with a loud trumpet call"	—	—
"sound of the trumpet"	"loud trumpet"	—	"trumpet will sound"
"dead in Christ will rise"	—	—	"dead will be raised"
"caught up together … to meet the Lord"	"gather his elect"	"assembling to meet him"	—
"in the clouds"	"on the clouds"	—	—
[When will this event occur?]	"immediately *after* the tribulation"	"that day will not come unless the rebellion comes *first*, and the man of lawlessness is *revealed*"	"at the *last* trumpet"

16

WHO MAKES THE U-TURN?

The Greek word for "meet" is *apantesis* (ap-an´-tay-sis). This word refers to the ancient practice of prominent citizens going out to welcome an approaching king or dignitary and escorting him back into the city. This way they could share in the glory of their visitor's arrival. Notice, the citizens *leave* the city, *meet* the dignitary, and then *return* with him to the city. The citizens change direction; the dignitary doesn't. He *continues on* to his destination. This is exactly how the word *apantesis* is used elsewhere in the Bible.

Matthew 25:6 describes the five wise virgins who go out to "meet" [*apantesis*] the bridegroom and then accompany him back to the marriage feast. Notice that it is the virgins who *turn around* after going out to meet the bridegroom. The bridegroom doesn't make a U-turn; he *continues on* to his destination.

Acts 28:15 describes how Christian brothers, hearing that St. Paul was approaching Rome, go outside the city to "meet" [*apantesis*] him and then escort him back into Rome. Again, notice that it is the Christian brothers who *turn around* after going out to meet Paul. Paul doesn't make a U-turn; he *continues on* to his destination. *Apantesis* is like picking someone up at an airport; it means to meet and *return with*, not meet and *leave with*.

Thus, when 1 Thessalonians 4:17 says all Christians will rise to meet [*apantesis*] Christ in the clouds, *Jesus* will not suddenly reverse course and sneak back to heaven. *Apantesis* means that *we* will turn around and escort Our King as He continues on to His destination: earth. 1 Thessalonians 4:17 is not describing a terrifying "left-behind" rapture. Rather, it is describing our glorious participation in Christ's Second Coming. We will rise up to meet Our Lord in the air and then share in His triumphant arrival as He takes possession of the earth and brings an end to human history.

References:

"It [*apantesis*] is used in the papyri [ordinary Greek writings] of a newly arriving magistrate. 'It seems that the special idea of the word was the official welcome of a newly arrived dignitary' (Moulton, *Greek Test. Gram.* Vol. I, 14)." W. E. Vine, *Vine's Complete Expository Dictionary of Old and New Testament Words* (Nashville, TN: Thomas Nelson Publishers, 1996), 402.

"The word seems to have been a kind of *technical term* for the official welcome of a newly arrived dignitary – a usage which accords excellently with its NT usage." J. H. Moulton and G. Milligan, *Vocabulary of the Greek New Testament* (Peabody, MA: Hendrickson Publishers, 1997), 53.

"The use of *apantesis* in 1 Thess. 4:17 is noteworthy. The ancient expression for the civic welcome of an important visitor or the triumphal entry of a new ruler into the capital city and thus to his reign is applied to Christ." Colin Brown, ed., *New International Dictionary of New Testament Theology* (Grand Rapids, MI: Zondervan, 1986), 325.

Also see Barbara R. Rossing, *The Rapture Exposed: The Message of Hope in the Book of Revelation* (Boulder, CO: Westview Press, 2004), 174–177.

➤ *Jesus' Public Ministry Is Accomplished*

Almost two thousand years ago, Jesus accomplished our redemption in a three-year public ministry. On Calvary Jesus, "knowing that all was now finished," said plainly, "It is finished" (John 19:28, 30). Why on earth (literally!) would He return for another public ministry, this one lasting for 1000 years? What is left to accomplish? He has already declared, "*I have overcome the world*" (John 16:33). In 1944, the Magisterium of the Catholic Church issued a statement condemning any form of millenarianism that teaches Christ will return and visibly reign on earth before the end of time. *CCC* repeats this condemnation in section 676.

> *The Church has rejected even modified forms of this falsification of the kingdom to come under the name of millenarianism ... (CCC 676).*

➤ *Overlooking Revelation 13*

Rapturists insist the saints will be raptured before the Antichrist and the tribulation. But Revelation 13:7–8 has the Antichrist (the Beast) waging war upon the saints *on earth*!

➤ *Misunderstanding Suffering*

Rapturists insist that believers will be snatched away to spare them the great trials of the tribulation. They fail to understand that the Bible teaches suffering is a privilege for the followers of Christ (Colossians 1:24, Romans 8:17–18). Jesus said His followers would have crosses to carry (Matthew 16:24) and that we would suffer in the world (John 16:33). In Acts 14:22 we are told, "through many tribulations we must enter the kingdom of God." Sacred Scripture is clear: to follow Christ is to share in His sufferings.

The early martyrs weren't raptured; later martyrs weren't raptured. The millions of saints brutally tortured by the communists in the 20th century weren't raptured. The Christians being crucified right now in the Sudan aren't being raptured. And Revelation 13 tells us the saints living during the Great Tribulation won't be raptured. In short, the view that believers will be spared the sufferings of the Great Tribulation is wishful thinking with no basis in Scripture. It is just another form of escapism packaged for a self-indulgent generation that rejects the value of suffering.

In summary, as we have shown in this article, the Dispensationalist view of the rapture is seriously flawed: it is unbiblical; it downgrades the role of the Church. It was unheard of until 1830. It is even rejected by most Protestants as a bizarre novelty. Like the Jehovah's Witnesses' teaching on the 144,000 people who go to heaven, or the Mormon teaching on the baptism of the dead, it is just another eccentric idea from 19th-century America!

---

4 Luke 17:37 adds an important detail. After Jesus declares that one man will be taken, the other left, and one woman will be taken, the other left, the disciples ask the obvious question: "Where, Lord?" Where will these people be taken? Jesus responds: "Where the body is, there the eagles [or vultures] will be gathered together." They are snatched away to a place of *death*, a place where carrion birds gather around carcasses. Christians definitely don't want to be snatched away in judgment.

PURGATORY

INTRODUCTION

Many Catholics have misconceptions about Purgatory. Some think Purgatory is like a "temporary hell" or that it's not taught in the Bible. Some hold that it's not a doctrine of the Church; others that it's virtually impossible to avoid.

Protestants strongly oppose the doctrine of Purgatory and frequently bring it up with Catholics. They are convinced Catholics cannot defend Purgatory from Sacred Scripture. Too often, Catholics prove them right by not even trying. In this section,[5] we will explain:

➤ Who goes to Purgatory

➤ How to defend Purgatory

➤ The nature of Purgatory

➤ How to avoid Purgatory

➤ Indulgences: what they are and how to defend them

The *CCC* makes the following points about Purgatory in sections 1030–1032:

① The existence of Purgatory is a doctrine.

② It is a place of purification for those who die imperfectly purified and thus need further purification after death.[6]

③ The purification of Purgatory is entirely different from the punishment of hell.

④ We can help the souls in Purgatory by our prayers and especially by offering the Holy Sacrifice of the Mass for them.

WHO GOES TO PURGATORY?

In order to defend the doctrine of Purgatory, we must explain two preliminary distinctions: between **guilt** and **punishment** and between **mortal** and **venial** sin.

Does God forgive the GUILT of sin and still require PUNISHMENT (reparation, atonement, expiation)?

Ask King David. In 2 Sam 12:13–14 we read:

> David said to Nathan, "I have sinned against the Lord." And Nathan said to David, "The Lord also has *put away your sin*; you shall not die. *Nevertheless*, because by this deed you have utterly scorned the Lord, *the child that is born to you shall die.*"

God forgave the *guilt* of David's sin, but He still required *reparation in the form of suffering*. A man might forgive a vandal for breaking his window, but still insist that he repair the damages.

---

5 Some material in this section appeared in our *Beginning Apologetics 1*, 30–33.

6 This would include those who die with the *guilt* of venial sin or with *punishment* remaining for venial and/or mortal sin. Those who die with the guilt of mortal sin obviously go to hell.

Where does Scripture distinguish between MORTAL and VENIAL sin?

1 John 5:16–17 proves degrees of sin, distinguishing between *deadly sin* and sin that is *not deadly*:

> If any one sees his brother committing what is not a mortal sin, he will ask, and God will give him life for those whose sin is not mortal. There is sin which is mortal; I do not say that one is to pray for that. All wrongdoing is sin, but there is sin which is not mortal.

James 1:14–15 reads:

> each person is tempted when he is lured and enticed by his own desire. Then desire when it has conceived gives birth to sin; and sin when it is full grown brings forth death.

St. James distinguishes desire from sin, and *beginning sin* from *mature sin* which brings death. Sin that kills the life of grace in the soul is **mortal.** Sin that only wounds and disfigures the soul is **venial.**

What if you die with only venial sins?

The souls of those who die in the perfect state of grace, without the least sin or reparation due to sin, go directly to heaven. The souls of those who die in the state of unrepented mortal (deadly) sin go directly to hell. What about the middle sort of people: *those who die in the state of grace, but with venial sin or with unpaid reparation due to forgiven sin*? They do not merit hell: they are still in the state of grace; yet they are not pure enough for heaven, where *"nothing unclean shall enter"* (Revelation 21:27).

Is Purgatory reasonable?

In 1769, James Boswell asked Samuel Johnson: "What do you think, Sir, of Purgatory, as believed by the Roman Catholics?" Johnson replied:

> Why, Sir, it is a very harmless doctrine. They are of the opinion that the generality of mankind are neither so obstinately wicked as to deserve everlasting punishment, nor so good as to merit being admitted into the society of the blessed spirits; and therefore that God is graciously pleased to allow a middle state, where they may be purified by certain degrees of suffering. You see, Sir, there is nothing unreasonable in this.

Though not a Catholic, Johnson could see that Purgatory was perfectly reasonable.

C. S. Lewis was another non-Catholic who believed in Purgatory. In his *Letters to Malcom: Chiefly on Prayer*, Lewis writes:

> Our souls *demand* Purgatory, don't they? Would it not break the heart if God said to us, "It is true, my son, that your breath smells and your rags drip with mud and slime, but we are charitable here and no one will upbraid you with these things, nor draw away from you. Enter into the joy"? Should we not say in reply, "With submission, sir, and if there is no objection, I'd *rather* be cleaned first." "It may hurt, you know." – "Even so, sir."

What does the Bible say about this?

God is perfect holiness.

> **Isaiah 6:3**: And one [seraphim] called to another and said: "Holy, holy, holy is the Lord of hosts."

We are called to that same holiness.

Matthew 5:48: You, therefore, must be perfect, as your heavenly Father is perfect.

1 Peter 1:15–16: as he who called you is holy, be holy yourselves in all your conduct; since it is written, "You shall be holy, for I am holy."

Without perfect holiness, we cannot see God in heaven.

Hebrews 12:14: Strive for peace with all men, and for the holiness without which no one will see the Lord.

Revelation 21:27: nothing unclean shall enter it [heaven].

What happens to the faithful who die without perfect holiness or with sin that is not deadly?

The biblical, logical, and historical answer is **Purgatory**.

Purgatory comes from the verb "purge" meaning "to purify or cleanse." We should keep this notion of *purification* in mind when explaining this doctrine.

What is the Catholic belief about Purgatory?

Purgatory is a temporary state of purification for the imperfect saints. The souls of the just who have died in the state of grace but with venial sins or with reparation due for forgiven sins are fully cleansed in Purgatory so that they may enter heaven. In Purgatory all remaining reparation for sin is made; all remaining self-love is purged and purified until only love of God remains.

REMEMBER THESE THREE POINTS:

① Only *imperfect saints in the state of grace* enter Purgatory. It is not a "second chance" for those who die in unrepented mortal sin.

② Purgatory exists for *purification* and *reparation*. The effects of sin are purged. The punishments due to sin are paid.

③ Purgatory is only *temporary*. Once the imperfect saints are purified they enter heaven. Everyone in Purgatory will go to heaven. Purgatory will cease to exist at the Second Coming. Only heaven and hell will remain eternally.

HOW DO WE DEFEND PURGATORY?

Is Purgatory scriptural?

First, we should note that the word "Purgatory" is not found in Sacred Scripture. This is not the point. The words "Trinity" and "Incarnation" are not found in Scripture, yet these doctrines are clearly taught there. Likewise, *the Bible teaches that an intermediate state of purification exists*. We call it Purgatory. What is important is the doctrine, not the name.

Where is the doctrine of Purgatory referred to in the Bible?

Matthew 12:32: And whoever says a word against the Son of man will be forgiven; but whoever speaks against the Holy Spirit will not be forgiven, either in this age *or in the age to come.*

Jesus implies that *some sins can be forgiven in the next world*. Sin cannot be forgiven in hell. There is no sin to be forgiven in heaven. Any remission of sin in the next world can only occur in Purgatory.

> **1 Corinthians 3:15:** If any man's work is burned up, he will suffer loss, though he himself will be saved, *but only as through fire.*

This cannot refer to eternal loss in hell, for there no one is saved. Nor can it refer to heaven, for there no one suffers. It refers, then, to a middle state where the soul temporarily suffers loss so that it may gain heaven. This is essentially the definition of Purgatory.

> **1 Peter 3:18–20:** For Christ also died for sins once for all, the righteous for the un-righteous, that he might bring us to God, being put to death in the flesh but made alive in the spirit; in which he went and preached to the *spirits in prison, who formerly did not obey*, when God's patience waited in the days of Noah, during the building of the ark, in which a few, that is, eight persons, were saved through water.
>
> **1 Peter 4:6:** For this is why the gospel was preached *even to the dead, that* though judged in the flesh like men, *they might live* in the spirit like God.

Note that it is a *prison for disobedient spirits*, and yet they were *saved* when Jesus preached to them. This is not hell, because no one is saved from hell. This is probably not the "limbo of the fathers," (often called "Abraham's bosom," where the righteous souls of the OT waited until Christ opened the gates of heaven), because this is a place for *disobedient* spirits. One cannot imagine that St. Peter is describing the waiting place of such righteous OT saints as David and John the Baptist when he mentions disobedient spirits.

St. Peter is describing a temporary state for disobedient souls who were eventually saved. *At the very least, it proves that a third place can exist between heaven and hell.* At the very most, it proves the Catholic doctrine of Purgatory.

The clearest affirmation of the existence of Purgatory comes from the Greek Septuagint: the Old Testament Scriptures used by Christ, all the NT writers, and the councils of Hippo and Carthage (which authoritatively determined the "canon" of inspired books of the Bible around ad 400).

> **2 Maccabees 12:42–45:** And the noble Judas exhorted the people to keep themselves free from sin, for they had seen with their own eyes what had happened because of the *sin of those who had fallen*. He also took up a collection, man by man, to the amount of two thousand drachmas of silver, and sent it to Jerusalem to provide for a sin offering. In doing this he acted *very well and honorably*, taking account of the resurrection. For if he were not expecting that those who had fallen would rise again, it would have been superfluous and foolish to pray for the dead. But if he was looking to the splendid reward that is laid up for those who fall asleep *in godliness*, it was a holy and pious thought. *Therefore he made atonement for the dead, that they might be delivered from their sin.*

This passage makes two important points:

① It proves the distinction between *mortal* and *venial* sin. Although these men had sinned by wearing tokens of foreign gods, they fell "asleep *in godliness.*" They sinned, yes, but still died in godliness so their sin had to be non-mortal, or venial. And venial sin, not mortal, is forgivable after death.

② It also proves the existence of a *middle state* where venial sins can be forgiven. We know it's impossible to aid souls in heaven (they have no need), and equally impossible to aid souls in hell (they have no hope). Praying for the dead presumes souls in a middle state where venial sins can be forgiven and atonement can be made.

This passage from Maccabees is a proof text. *It explicitly affirms an intermediate state where the faithful departed make atonement for their non-mortal sins.* Martin Luther's reaction demonstrates the strength of this passage. It was so contrary to his "justification by faith alone" theology that he removed 2 Maccabees, along with six other books, from his Old Testament.

This takes us to the question of the canon of the Bible: How do we know which books *really* constitute the Bible? *By whose authority* do we trust that the books upon which we stake our eternal salvation really are inspired?

Do we rely on the private judgment of Luther, who also wanted to throw out Esther, James and Revelation, and thought nothing of adding the word "alone" to his translation of Romans 3:28?

Or, do we accept the divinely protected judgment of the Catholic Church who used her authority around the year AD 400 to determine the official canon of the Bible? This is the same Bible (minus the seven books removed by Luther) Protestants use to attack the very authority of the Church who gave it to them.

Even if one rejects 2 Maccabees as Scripture, there can be no doubt that, as history, the book accurately reflects the religious character of the Jews of the second century BC. A little more than one hundred years before Christ, Jews prayed for their dead (and still do to this day).

Some of the earliest Christian liturgies (worship services) include prayers for the dead. Ancient Christian tomb inscriptions from the second and third centuries frequently contain an appeal for prayers for the dead.[7] This practice makes sense only if early Christians believed in Purgatory even if they did not use that name for it.

Tertullian, writing in the year AD 211, presents the practice of praying and sacrificing for the dead as an established

---

7 The epitaph of Abercius [AD 180] reads: "The citizen of a prominent city, I erected this while I lived, that I might have a resting place for my body. Abercius is my name, a disciple of the chaste shepherd who feeds his sheep on the mountains and in the fields, who has great eyes surveying everywhere, who taught me the faithful writings of life. Standing by, I, Abercius, ordered this to be inscribed; truly I was in my seventy-second year. *May everyone who is in accord with this and who understands it pray for Abercius*" (Jurgens, #187).

8 *The Crown*, 3, 3; Jurgens, #367.

custom: "We offer *sacrifices for the dead on their birthday anniversaries.*"[8] This practice of praying for the dead was universal among Christians for fifteen centuries before the Reformation.

Are there any New Testament passages that refer to prayers and practices performed for the benefit of the deceased?

> **2 Timothy 1:16–18:** May the Lord grant mercy to the household of Onesiphorus, for he often refreshed me; he was not ashamed of my chains … may the Lord grant him to find mercy from the Lord on that Day.

St. Paul prays for his departed friend Onesiphorus, which makes sense only if he can be helped by prayer.

> **1 Corinthians 15:29:** Otherwise, what do people mean by being *baptized on behalf of the dead*? If the dead are not raised at all, why are people baptized on their behalf?

In his argument for the resurrection of the body, St. Paul mentions (without condemning or approving) the practice of people being baptized for the benefit of the dead, who cannot be helped if there is no intermediate state of purification.[9]

In short, if the Jews, St. Paul, and the early Christians prayed for the dead, we

should have no fear of praying for them as well. Praying for the dead *presumes an intermediate state of purification*, whatever you may call it. Catholics call it Purgatory.

St. Peter, addressing born-again Christians who are undergoing trials, tells them that their sufferings are purifying their faith like fire purifies gold (1 Peter 1:6–7). Hebrews chapters 5–13 is an extended passage describing how trials lead to spiritual growth. Our everyday experience shows us faithful Christians who endure trials that make them holier: more patient, more just, more charitable. In this world, Christians are continually called to remove obstacles keeping them from perfect holiness. Some faithful people die before they are totally purified. Thus, they need some other place to complete the purifying process before they can enter heaven.

WHAT IS THE NATURE OF PURGATORY?

Although there are plenty of books on Purgatory, few address the *nature* of Purgatory. What is it like? What kind of suffering is involved? What is the attitude

of souls there? How does it compare with hell, earth, and heaven?

There are two outstanding books on the nature of Purgatory. The first is the *Treatise on Purgatory*[10] by

---

[9] On the grounds of sola scriptura, Protestants have no way to refute the Mormon practice of baptism for the dead, which is based on this passage. They must use the early Church Fathers and Church Tradition to prove that Christianity never endorsed this practice.

[10] Some translations refer to it as *Purgation and Purgatory*.

St. Catherine of Genoa (1447–1510). Our Lord gave St. Catherine deep knowledge of Purgatory. He also let her experience its sufferings for several years while on earth. Orthodox theologians consider her book to be a standard reference.

The greatest description of the purifications a soul must endure to reach spiritual perfection is the *Dark Night of the Soul* by St. John of the Cross (1542–1591). Book two treats the trials of the spirit which St. John describes as similar to the sufferings of Purgatory.

We will use these two classics, together with the *CCC* and Doctors of the Church, in the following discussion of Purgatory.

Since souls in Purgatory are in the state of grace, they are assured of going to heaven. In addition, they have perfect charity. They are without sin and are incapable of sinning. They commit no imperfections. They are totally free of the *guilt* of sin. If they died with unforgiven venial sins, the guilt was immediately removed at the moment of death, when they entered into perfect charity. Only the remaining *punishment* of sin is taken to Purgatory. At the moment of death, they are given some indication of the glory that awaits them in heaven. We must always remember that the souls in Purgatory are *saints*. They have won the eternal crown of glory. They will take their place among the blessed of heaven.

Purgatory is aptly described as a place of stillness, a place of twilight. Souls in Purgatory have no bodies to distract them. They are no longer tempted in any way as they were in this world of pilgrimage. They no longer worry about death and judgment; all that is behind them. They have no earthly cares such as family or job obligations. They no longer worry about "getting ahead." Nor are they concerned about gaining eternal merit.[11] Souls in Purgatory are focused. They have only one purpose: to remove any remaining punishment for sin.

Purgatory is like twilight. Many people wake up early to pray in morning twilight. All is still; there are no distractions. They can focus completely on God. Although it is dim, they have a glimpse of light because the sun will soon rise on the horizon.

In Purgatory, there are no distractions of any kind. Souls focus entirely on God, for whom they long. They are in darkness (suffering) because they still have an obstacle (the punishments due to sin) that prevents them from receiving the sunlight (the Beatific Vision[12]). However, God manifests His love for them in a consoling, comforting way (the predawn light).

---

11 There is no gaining merit in Purgatory. The degree of glory we will have for eternity is determined the moment we die. Whatever spiritual treasure we have at the moment of death determines the degree of glory we will have in heaven. We can no longer merit in Purgatory. In other words, in Purgatory we cannot increase the glory we will have in heaven.

12 The Beatific Vision is the direct contemplation of God in His heavenly glory (*CCC*, 1028).

St. Catherine of Genoa stresses that although souls in Purgatory suffer much, they have peace and joy. They have gained their salvation; they love God perfectly; and they know that He loves them infinitely. At death, God gives souls a glimpse of heaven. They see God as the Supreme Good; they love Him; they want to be with Him. But they are detained until they fully atone for their sins. This is the chief suffering of Purgatory: souls yearn to be with God and suffer because they cannot yet enter into His presence.

During their earthly lives, saints longed for God and suffered because they couldn't possess Him directly in the Beatific Vision. St. Teresa of Avila was given a glimpse of heaven. She suffered so intensely she exclaimed, "I die because I don't die!" But she was also flooded with peace and joy because she saw how much God loved her and how well-founded her hope of being with Him in heaven was.

Many Christians suffer with great peace and joy because they know trials can draw them closer to God. Likewise, the souls in Purgatory suffer with peace and joy because they also know their sufferings are bringing them ever nearer to God. They know God's purifying love is burning away all the obstacles keeping them from heaven.

Here's another way of understanding the suffering in Purgatory. Imagine Patient Y with an incurable cancer that burns like fire. He has no hope for a cure. The searing pain has no benefit. Patient Y will suffer with great despondency, knowing the pointless agony will not end until death.

Now imagine Patient Z with *curable* cancer. The doctor begins a treatment that causes him to suffer as much as Patient Y. But the doctor assures Patient Z that the painful treatment is only targeting cancer cells; not a single healthy cell will be harmed. Patient Z will gladly suffer the same searing pain with peace and joy. He knows the treatment will kill his cancer, restore his health, and stop the pain.

Souls in hell (Patient Y) suffer great torments that have no healing purpose and will never end. Souls in Purgatory (Patient Z) suffer torment, but their sufferings only attack the imperfections that keep them from perfect spiritual health (heaven). Once the imperfections are burned away the pain will cease. That is why they suffer with peace and joy.

> *The Church gives the name Purgatory to this final purification of the elect,* **which is entirely different from the punishment of the damned** *(CCC 1031).*

Many people have the misconception that when souls go to Purgatory, they are desperately trying to get into heaven, but God drags them kicking and screaming into Purgatory. The truth is the opposite. Heaven has no gates! Souls go to Purgatory willingly, even eagerly.

When people die in the state of grace, but needing further purification, they immediately realize they cannot enter heaven because they have put up obstacles through their own free will. They could and should have removed these obstacles in this life. They perceive that God lovingly provides a place to complete their purification. Souls enter Purgatory freely, grateful for God's mercy. They accept the necessary purification with joyful submission to God's will.

As we can see, the pains of Purgatory are totally different from the sufferings of hell (*CCC* 1031). To view Purgatory as a "temporary hell" is a serious misunderstanding. Souls in hell are *damned*. They suffer eternal torment in utter despair, completely devoid of love. Souls in Purgatory are *saints*. They suffer purifying pain full of hope and love since they know they will soon be fully united to God in heaven.

How Can We Avoid Purgatory?

Our goal should be to go straight to heaven when we die. "Just making it to Purgatory" is a foolish aim. We can entirely avoid the immense suffering of Purgatory if we learn and do those things that will keep us out.

We must avoid two extremes. One is *despair*. Many Catholics mistakenly believe that since they aren't Mother Teresa or John Paul II, they'll have to spend a long time in Purgatory. However, this pessimism contradicts the teaching of the great saints. There are easy ways to avoid Purgatory completely. Anyone, no matter how sinful, can do it.

Remember, many people, after a lifetime of sin, were baptized on their deathbeds. Since baptism wipes out both the guilt and punishment of sin, these people went straight to heaven. It doesn't make any sense for God to let a wicked person who converts on his deathbed avoid Purgatory, but make it virtually impossible for a righteous person to do the same. Moreover, millions of people die before the age of reason and so avoid Purgatory. One doesn't have to be Mother Teresa or John Paul II to go straight to heaven.

The other extreme is *presumption*. This is the unfounded confidence that God wouldn't possibly let *me* suffer in Purgatory. God loves me; thus, *I* don't have to worry about it. This assumption might not only lead me to Purgatory, but could very well land me in hell.

The following are easy ways to avoid Purgatory:

① **Daily prayer**. Each day, ask God to give you the grace to enter heaven immediately upon death. As the Bible teaches, God answers persevering prayer (Luke 18:1–8).

② **Frequent confession**. Going to confession regularly helps us avoid sin. Each confession removes much of the temporal punishment due to sin. A devout confession can remove it all!

③ **Frequent Mass and Holy Communion**. Attending Mass and receiving communion devoutly removes much of the punishment due to sin, and may even remove it all. If you are serious about avoiding Purgatory, attend as many weekday Masses as possible.

④ **Regular penance**. Daily self-denial is an excellent way to atone for sins. Some examples include fasting, going without dessert or TV, giving to charity, and making more time for prayer.

⑤ **Daily rosary**. Our Lady gave 15 promises to St. Dominic and Blessed Alan de la Roche for those who pray the rosary. The 9th is Mary's promise to deliver from Purgatory those who are devoted to the rosary. Praying five decades of the rosary every day is a sure way to develop this devotion.

⑥ **Offering up your death** and all its circumstances entirely to God.

⑦ **Offering up your daily crosses**— pains, burdens, and duties— completely to God. Death and daily crosses will happen to us anyway. Why not make a virtue of necessity and avoid Purgatory in the process? The saints have assured us that sincerely making these two offerings will keep us out of Purgatory, provided we are otherwise leading a good Catholic life.

⑧ **The sacrament of anointing**. In addition to helping us endure illness in union with Christ (see ⑦ at left), this sacrament takes away the temporal punishment of sin. If you are in the state of grace, you don't need to go to confession before receiving anointing. But confessing before anointing will maximize the removal of punishment due for sin and heighten the other spiritual and physical benefits of this sacrament.

⑨ **Indulgences**. Learn about indulgences and how to get them. We will cover this in the next section.

These are some of the ordinary ways to avoid Purgatory. As you can see, they are not hard. In the next section we will discuss indulgences. We will see that they, too, are powerful and easy ways to help us go straight to heaven.

INDULGENCES

The two consequences of sin are *guilt* and *punishment*. Guilt is removed when our sins are forgiven. But punishment due to forgiven sin often remains. If we die in the state of grace, but still have any punishment due for sin, we must expiate (atone for, make satisfaction for) that punishment in Purgatory. To help us eliminate all temporal punishment while on earth, the Church grants indulgences.[13] An indulgence is the "remission before God of the temporal punishment due to sins whose guilt has already been forgiven" (*CCC* 1471).

Jesus gave His Catholic Church the power to forgive sins (John 20:23) as well as the power to bind and loose (Matthew 18:18). In addition, Christ made His Church the steward of the merits He won for us through His life, death, and resurrection. To this infinite spiritual treasury, God adds the merits that the saints gained by cooperating with His grace. The Church, as a good mother, uses this spiritual treasure to help her children remove the punishment due for sin while at the same time encouraging them to grow in holiness.

> *An indulgence is a remission before God of the temporal punishment due to sins whose guilt has already been forgiven, which the faithful Christian who is duly disposed gains under certain prescribed conditions through the action of the Church which, as the minister of redemption, dispenses and applies with authority the treasury of the satisfaction of Christ and the saints (CCC 1471).*

> *An indulgence is partial or plenary according as it removes either part or all of the temporal punishment due to sin (CCC 1471).*

Indulgences granted by the Church are either partial or plenary. A *partial* indulgence removes some of the punishment due for sins. A *plenary* indulgence removes all of it. We can gain indulgences for ourselves or for souls in Purgatory, but not for other people living on earth.[14]

> *The faithful can gain indulgences for themselves or apply them to the dead (CCC 1471).*

[13] An indulgence is not a permission to *indulge* in sin, but a remission of some or all of the punishment due to sin. Indulgences do not pardon sin. Sins must be forgiven by repentance and confession, and one must be in the state of grace to gain an indulgence. Then and only then may one gain a remission of temporal penalties for those forgiven sins.

[14] For the living, the indulgence gained is by way of absolution. For the dead, the indulgence gained is by way of *intercession*.

Make sure the books you read on indulgences are written after 1968, the year the Church revised its regulations. Before 1968, books on gaining indulgences would specify a certain number of days associated with various good works. This didn't mean that this indulgence took away that number of days in Purgatory. It simply meant that the indulgence gained by a particular work was equal to the indulgence gained by doing a public penance in the early Church for that number of days. In 1968, the Church simplified this and now categorizes indulgences as either partial or plenary.

For many years, it was assumed that to gain a plenary indulgence, you had to go to confession within 8 days before or after the indulgenced act. However, on January 29, 2000, the Apostolic Penitentiary issued a document that suggests about 20 days before or after, which is roughly three weeks. Thus, if you go to confession at least every six weeks, you could gain a plenary indulgence every day!

> *To understand this doctrine and practice of the Church, it is necessary to understand that sin has a* double consequence. *Grave sin deprives us of communion with God and therefore makes us incapable of eternal life, the privation of which is called the "eternal punishment" of sin. On the other hand every sin, even venial, entails an unhealthy attachment to creatures, which must be purified either here on earth, or after death in the state called Purgatory. This purification frees one from what is called the "temporal punishment" of sin. These two punishments must not be conceived of as a kind of vengeance inflicted by God from without, but as following from the very nature of sin. A conversion which proceeds from a fervent charity can attain the complete purification of the sinner in such a way that no punishment would remain* (CCC, 1472).

HOW DO WE DEFEND INDULGENCES?

Many Protestants have a knee-jerk reaction against indulgences. They remember Martin Luther's well-known conflict with the monk Johann Tetzel over the selling of indulgences.[15] In reality, indulgences shouldn't be controversial. To understand indulgences, these Protestants need to jettison their historical and emotional baggage and look at the facts objectively.

The crucial issue here is the forgiveness of sins. Sin has two consequences—*guilt* and *temporal punishment*. We must be free of both to enter heaven. Of the two, guilt is far more dangerous. The guilt of a single mortal sin will send us to hell if it isn't removed before we die. But no amount of temporal punishment will send us to hell; it can only delay our entrance into heaven.

Jesus gave His Church the power to forgive sin. This power is implied in Matthew 18:18 and explicitly given in John 20:23. If the Church is able to forgive sin, why should this power be limited to guilt? Why wouldn't it also include the power to forgive temporal punishment, the other immediate consequent of sin?

> 📖 **Matthew 18:18:** Truly, I say to you, whatever you bind on earth shall be bound in heaven, and whatever you loose on earth shall be loosed in heaven.
>
> 📖 **John 20:22–23:** he breathed on them, and said to them, 'Receive the Holy Spirit. If you forgive the sins of any, they are forgiven; if you retain the sins of any, they are retained.

Guilt can be eternal (forever). Temporal punishment, by definition, is only temporary (for a time). Removing guilt is superior to removing temporal punishment. It doesn't make sense that the Church has the far

---

15 It is absolutely wrong to sell indulgences. The Church has always taught that indulgences cannot be purchased and has never sanctioned their sale. True, there were many abuses, but the Church took strong measures to end them. It is unfair to blame the entire Catholic Church for the unauthorized actions of people like Tetzel.

In 1514, Pope Leo X (1513–1521) granted certain indulgences to those who would give alms toward the building of St. Peter's Basilica in Rome. But the indulgence was granted for the *charitable work*, not for the *money*, and only upon fulfilling the prescribed conditions. Indulgences are never obtained by mere money, but by doing good works—prayer, fasting, and almsgiving—with the proper disposition. The money doesn't buy an indulgence. However, giving money for some charitable purpose can *gain* the giver an indulgence. Remember, Jesus gave a special blessing to the widow who gave her mite as alms to the temple (Mark 12:41–44; Luke 21:1–4). But the widow didn't "buy" Jesus' blessing for a mite. He rewarded her for her good deed and pure heart. Likewise, the Church can and does grant indulgences for our good deeds, including almsgiving. We're not purchasing something of equal value; it's not an economic exchange. We're doing a good deed: giving alms to some charitable cause. And Christ, through His Church, rewards that good deed—depending on our purity of heart—with the blessing of reduced temporal punishment.

greater power of forgiving the guilt of sin but lacks the far lesser power of forgiving the punishment due for sin. Remember, God gave the Church the keys of the kingdom of heaven. This logically includes power over the punishment due for sin, since this punishment keeps us from going straight to heaven.

Many Protestants, including many Fundamentalists, believe as Catholics do that baptism prepares a person to immediately enter heaven. Thus, they share the Catholic belief that baptism wipes away both the guilt and punishment of sin. These Protestants believe that the Church, through their ministers, *can* remove both the guilt *and* punishment of sin. So they agree with Catholics in principle: the Church *does* have the power to remove punishment as well as guilt.

One final point: Christ gave the Church the power to "bind and loose." What biblical reason is there to say that the power to bind and loose does not extend to punishment? Without a strong biblical argument to the contrary, we should rather believe that the Church with the greater power of removing the guilt of sin also has the lesser power of removing the punishment due to sin.

HOW CAN WE GAIN A PARTIAL INDULGENCE?

In a partial indulgence, the Church, out of its spiritual treasury, grants a remission of *some* of the temporal punishment due to our forgiven sins. To get a partial indulgence, we must be baptized, in the state of grace, and not excommunicated. In addition, we must have the intention of receiving the partial indulgence. There is no limit to the number of partial indulgences we may receive.

The Bible mentions several ways to atone for sins: prayer, good deeds, almsgiving, and fasting.

> **Proverbs 16:6:** By loyalty and faithfulness iniquity is atoned for, and by the fear of the Lord a Man avoids evil.

> **Daniel 4:24–7:** Therefore, O king, let my counsel be acceptable to you; break off your sins by practicing righteousness, and your iniquities by showing mercy to the oppressed, that there may perhaps be a lengthening of your tranquility.

> **Tobit 12:8–9:** *Prayer* is good when accompanied by *fasting*, *almsgiving*, and *righteousness*. ... For *almsgiving* delivers from death, and it will purge away every sin. Those who perform *deeds of charity* and of *righteousness* will have fullness of life....

> **Matthew 6:1–18:** when you give *alms* ... when you *pray* ... when you *fast* ... [do so] in secret; and your Father who sees in secret will reward you.

> **Acts 10:4:** Your *prayers* and *your alms* have ascended as a memorial before God.

Accordingly, the following are the three ordinary ways to get a partial indulgence:

➢ Saying a short prayer in the midst of our daily duties. The prayer can be silent or out loud; it can be in our own words or memorized. Some suggested prayers[16] include:

a. Sign of the cross
b. Morning offering
c. Act of contrition
d. Act of faith
e. Act of hope
f. Act of love
g. Guardian Angel prayer
h. Anima Christi
i. Apostles' Creed
j. Litany of the Sacred Heart
k. Litany of the Blessed Virgin
l. Memorare
m. Any prayer for vocations
n. Five decades of the Rosary

➢ Doing some direct act of charity like feeding the hungry, helping the sick, giving clothing to the needy, comforting the sorrowful, or instructing someone in the truths of the faith (in short, performing any of the corporal or spiritual works of mercy).[17]

---

16 See Appendix: Suggested Prayers on p. 39.
17 The seven corporal works of mercy are: feeding the hungry, giving drink to the thirsty, clothing the naked, sheltering the homeless, visiting the sick, visiting the imprisoned, and burying the dead. The seven spiritual works of mercy are: counseling the doubtful, instructing the ignorant, admonishing sinners, comforting the afflicted, forgiving offenses, bearing wrongs patiently, and praying for the living and the dead.

➤ Abstaining from some permissible good; for example: giving up a meal, a dessert, or a favorite TV program.

We can also obtain a partial indulgence by the following special actions:

① Visiting Our Lord in the Blessed Sacrament for any length of time.

② Visiting a cemetery and praying for the poor souls in Purgatory.

③ Devoutly wearing or displaying a crucifix, rosary, scapular, or holy medal.

④ Teaching or studying Catholic doctrine for any length of time.

Remember, to gain a partial indulgence, we must express an intention to gain it (either silently or vocally). Once we make an intention to gain a partial indulgence through a particular prayer or action, that intention remains for each subsequent prayer or action. However, it is a good practice to renew the intention from time to time.

HOW CAN WE GAIN A PLENARY INDULGENCE?

A plenary indulgence takes away *all* the temporal punishment due to sin. To gain a plenary indulgence, we must be baptized, in the state of grace, and not excommunicated. These are the same conditions for gaining a partial indulgence. In addition, we must be free from any *attachment to sin*, whether mortal or venial. This means we are truly struggling against anything in our lives that we know is sinful in any way.

THE FOLLOWING ARE THE FOUR ORDINARY WAYS TO GAIN A PLENARY INDULGENCE:

① Spending 30 minutes before the Blessed Sacrament.

② Spending 30 minutes reading Sacred Scripture for devotional purposes.

③ Making the Stations of the Cross.

④ Saying a public rosary. This would include saying a rosary in a religious group, in a family, or if alone, in a church aloud or at least in a whisper.

Each time we do one of these four works for a plenary indulgence, we must receive communion and say some prayers for the intentions of the Pope (an Our Father and a Hail Mary will do). Also, we must go to confession within 20 days either before or after.[18] This means that if we go to confession every six weeks, we can gain a plenary indulgence every day. We may only get one plenary indulgence a day unless we are dying. This is different from a partial indulgence, which has no daily limit.

Remember, to gain either a partial or plenary indulgence, we must make an intention to do so.

---

[18] One sacramental confession suffices for numerous plenary indulgences, but a separate Holy Communion and a separate prayer for the Holy Father's intentions are required for each plenary indulgence.

HEAVEN

Sacred Scripture, the saints, and the Church all teach that we should long for our heavenly homeland with joyful hope. Yearning for heaven gives us strength and courage in this land of exile. To properly desire heaven, we must first correctly understand it. Then our thinking will be theologically sound and spiritually fruitful.

To understand our life in heaven, we must first understand what a great privilege it is to be human. God made us in His own image and likeness. We can know and love. We are able to receive God's own divine life—grace—into our souls. We are called to be (and are transformed into) God's children in this life. Heaven is our final destiny. There, everything we were made for reaches its perfect fulfillment. In heaven, we will fully realize how precious a gift God gave us in creating us in His image.

In this life, we are led by different lights. The light of bodily vision enables us to see the world around us. The light of reason enables us to discover truth. The light of faith enables us to accept the mysteries of God's Kingdom even when they are beyond our reason and senses.

This perfect life with the Most Holy Trinity— this communion of life and love with the Trinity, with the Virgin Mary, the angels and all the blessed—is called "heaven." Heaven is the ultimate end and fulfillment of the deepest human longings, the state of supreme, definitive happiness (CCC, 1024).

In heaven we will receive the final light, the light of glory, which enables us to see God face-to-face and to comprehend truth with unimaginable power. The Light of Glory makes possible the Beatific Vision: God directly infusing us with His truth, love, and life. The light of glory and the transfiguration of our bodies and souls in heaven will equip us for inconceivable spiritual joys. In heaven there will be no longings or desires, because everything we were made for will be fully and perfectly fulfilled.

It is important not to view heaven as just earthly life *perfected*. Many Christians and non-Christians make this mistake. Heavenly life is a way of being, knowing, and loving that surpasses all earthly experiences. "No eye has seen, nor ear heard, nor the heart of man conceived, what God has prepared for those who love him" (1 Corinthians 2:9).

Imagine a man born blind who studied the physical properties of light. If he were at the Grand Canyon at sunset, and his sight was miraculously restored, he would gasp at the beauty before him. All his scientific knowledge would pale before his direct vision. Something similar will happen when we leave this earthly life of grace in faith, and enter the heavenly life of grace in glory.

Although the essence of heaven is the Beatific Vision—the immediate contemplation of God in all His glory—there will be additional joys. We will be reunited with relatives and friends and enjoy fellowship with all the other saints. In the light of glory we will know them and love them immeasurably better than we could in this life. Our bodies will have powers, abilities, and uses far beyond any in this world.

Think of a baby in his mother's womb. His hands are useful for moving, for steadying himself, even sucking. Imagine him thinking: what else could I possibly do with my hands; how could there be higher and better purpose? In the womb, he simply couldn't conceive of playing a piano concerto or performing delicate brain surgery. But unimaginably better uses await his hands outside the womb. Likewise, inconceivably better uses await our bodies outside this earthly life.

An additional joy of heaven will be the New Heaven and the New Earth. All creation will share the glorification of our bodies (Romans 8:19–23). The universe will be transformed into a new condition of perfection, beauty, majesty, and glory. If we marvel at the beauty of a magnificent sunset or snow-capped mountain in this world, imagine the beauty that awaits us in the New Heaven and the New Earth.

One caution: when we speak of heaven as being the land of eternal rest, we do not mean rest in terms of inactivity. What we rest from are trials, sufferings, longings, imperfections, sin, and death. Heaven will be a place of ecstatic experiences and amazing adventures.

Knowing that our delights in heaven will never end will only increase our joy. In this temporal world, we experience our imperfect and fleeting joys one moment at a time. In heaven we will experience *all* our heavenly delights in one eternal *now*!

HELL

The *CCC* gives this definition of hell: "To die in mortal sin without repenting and accepting God's merciful love means remaining separated from him for ever by our own free choice. This state of definitive self-exclusion from communion with God and the blessed is called 'hell'" (1033). Heaven is permanent and perfect communion *with* God. Hell is permanent and horrific separation *from* God.

Before the general resurrection, only the soul suffers in hell. After the resurrection, the body will be reunited with the soul and will share its misery. There are two torments of hell: the physical and the spiritual. The greatest suffering will be the loss (and full knowledge of the loss) of the Beatific Vision—not being able to know and love God face-to-face.

Jesus describes hell as "eternal fire"[19] (Matthew 25:41) where the torment is so severe that the damned grind their teeth in agony (Matthew 8:12). The utter despair and the severe remorse and guilt of conscience are vividly described in Luke 16:19–13 (the rich man and Lazarus) and Mark 9:48 where hell is called a place where "the worm does not die." This latter expression is generally believed to refer to the unquenchable pangs of conscience that characterize the damned in hell.

Two famous descriptions of hell are found in St. Theresa of Avila's autobiography (chapter 32) and the vision of hell shown to the Fatima children by Our Lady. Each graphically portrays the unending physical and spiritual torments of hell. For those who believe in hell, a brief mediation of its terrors suffices. For those whose hearts are closed, no amount of frightening detail will move them. Unfortunately, if they end up in hell and experience its reality firsthand, it will be too late to avoid it.

We can also consider hell in terms of fulfillment. Just as heaven is the fulfillment of all we were made for, hell is the loss of everything we were made for. For humans, heaven isn't just the greatest goal; it's the *only* goal. If we lose heaven, we lose everything. Apart from heaven, we have absolutely no purpose. Hell is total failure, utter loss.

In John 15, Jesus gives us the parable of the vine and the branches. The branches have a beautiful purpose: to produce grapes. But interestingly, if the branches are cut off from the vine, they have no other use. They are too soft and crooked for construction. They can't even be used in the fireplace for heat—they give off too much smoke! As Our Lord says, they are good for nothing but to be burned as useless trash. Likewise, as Jesus suggests in this parable, to lose the kingdom of heaven is to lose all purpose and meaning. The only thing that remains is eternal frustration and agony.

---

[19] Out of the entire dictionary, Jesus deliberately picked the word "fire" to describe the searing pains of hell.

ANSWERING OBJECTIONS TO HELL

➤ *How can anyone possibly believe in hell?*

Because God Himself teaches that hell exists. Throughout the Gospels, Jesus continually warns us about the real possibility of going to hell: "it is better that you lose one of your members than that your whole body be thrown into hell" (Matthew 5:29); "do not fear those who kill the body … fear him who, after he has killed, has power to cast into hell" (Luke 12:4–5). At the Last Judgment, Jesus will say to the unrighteous, "Depart from me, you cursed, into the eternal fire prepared for the devil and his angels" and "they will go away into eternal punishment" (Matthew 25:41, 46).

➤ *How could a merciful God send someone to hell for all eternity?*

God respects our free will. If we freely choose to reject God by mortal sin, and persist in rejecting Him and all His mercy and grace until death, what is God supposed to do: drag us kicking, screaming, and defiantly disobeying into heaven? God is a gentleman; He's not going to *force* us to be with Him if we don't want to. God doesn't send anyone to hell. A person sends *himself* there by freely setting his will against God's. At death, this setting of the will becomes permanent. Those who are permanently turned against God get what they want: permanent separation from God, which is hell. As C.S. Lewis observed, the gates of hell are locked from the *inside*. If the damned would ever turn toward God they would be saved; but they will not. They stubbornly fix their wills forever against Him.

➤ *But punishing someone forever in hell is vindictive and cruel.*

Just as God doesn't send anyone to hell—people freely send themselves—so God doesn't cause suffering in hell. A convicted felon in prison isn't being directly tortured by the state. He's lost his freedom because of his own free actions. The lack of freedom—which men naturally long for—is prison's chief torment. Similarly, the lack of God's presence—which men are made for—is hell's chief torment.

Remember, God made us. We need Him.[20] *With* Him, in heaven, we will be totally fulfilled. *Without* Him, in hell, we will be totally frustrated. Permanently rejecting God means permanently rejecting all happiness, love, goodness, and peace. Permanently rejecting God means permanently hurting ourselves. God *allows* us to suffer the results of rejecting Him, but He certainly doesn't directly will or cause those results.

➤ *But how could a temporary sin merit eternal punishment?*

Even in this life, many temporary actions have permanent consequences. Someone who plucks out his eyes is permanently blind. Someone who commits suicide is permanently dead. One car wreck can permanently paralyze. One act of adultery can permanently ruin a marriage. So why is it hard to imagine that temporary sins in this life might have eternal consequences?

20 As St. Augustine so accurately perceived, "You have made us for Yourself, O Lord, and our hearts are restless until they rest in You."

Mortal sin kills the supernatural life of grace in our souls. If we die in that state, our souls are permanently dead. If we don't repent from mortal sins, we commit spiritual suicide.

➢ *How can* momentary *disobedience* permanently *fix our wills against God?*

Life is a test, to see if we will choose to love and obey God. Most tests have a time limit. When time expires, the scores become permanent. In the test of life, the time limit is death. At death, the time to choose comes to an end. "We must work the works of him who sent me, while it is day; night comes, when no one can work" (John 9:4). At death, our decisions and works become permanent.

Until time expires, we can always change our answers. At any moment we can reject God. At any moment we can convert and accept God. "When the righteous turns from his righteousness, and commits iniquity, he shall die for it. And when the wicked turns from his wickedness, and does what is lawful and right, he shall live by it" (Ezekiel 33:18–19). We can overturn a lifetime of righteousness with a single mortal sin. We can overturn a lifetime of wickedness with a single act of repentance. With every choice, our eternal destiny hangs in the balance. But when life ends, our choices in time (good or bad) become fixed in eternity.

MARY & THE END TIMES

To appreciate Mary's role in the end times more fully, we encourage you to read *Beginning Apologetics 6: How to Explain and Defend Mary*. In this booklet, we show from Sacred Scripture and

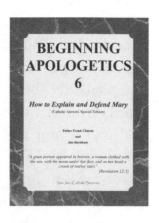

the Church Fathers that Mary is the New Eve, the New Testament (NT) Ark of the Covenant, and the NT Queen Mother. We also show that Mary is clearly the spiritual mother of Jesus' followers (Revelation 12:17). In addition, we show that Mary is the "woman" of Revelation 12, who plays a monumental role in the climactic battle of Christ and His followers against the Dragon and his followers.

St. Louis De Monfort's classic, *True Devotion to the Blessed Virgin Mary*, contains a section entitled "Mary's Special Part in the Last Days: Prophetic Views." Here, he gives a stirring account of Mary's mission in the end times,

beautifully and powerfully presenting her as the Woman of Revelation 12. We recommend reading this section of *True Devotion* to understand Mary's profound role in the end times.

Revelation 12:1–17: And a great portent appeared in heaven, a woman clothed with the sun, with the moon under her feet, and on her head a crown of twelve stars; she was with child and … she brought forth a male child, one who is to rule all the nations with a rod of iron…. Then the dragon was angry with the woman, and went off to make war on the rest of her offspring, on those who keep the commandments of God and bear testimony to Jesus.

Even though Sacred Scripture clearly assigns Mary a major role in the end times, one can read numerous Dispensationalist books on the rapture and the end times that never mention her *once*. In their end times theology, Mary is totally non-existent. This position is completely unbiblical.

APPENDIX: SUGGESTED PRAYERS

The Sign of the Cross

In the name of the Father, and of the Son, and of the Holy Spirit. Amen.

Morning Offering

O Jesus, through the Immaculate Heart of Mary, I offer You all my prayers, works, joys, and sufferings of this day, in union with the holy sacrifice of the Mass throughout the world, in reparation for our sins, for the intentions of our associates, and especially for the intentions of the Holy Father for the month of ____. Amen.

Act of Contrition

O my God, I am heartily sorry for having offended Thee, and I detest all my sins, because I dread the loss of heaven and the pains of hell; but most of all because they offend Thee, my God, Who art all good and worthy of all my love. I firmly resolve, with the help of Thy grace, to sin no more and to avoid the near occasions of sin. Amen.

Act of Faith

O my God, I firmly believe that Thou art one God in three divine Persons, Father, Son, and Holy Spirit; I believe that Thy divine Son became man and died for our sins, and that He shall come to judge the living and the dead. I believe these and all the truths that the holy Catholic Church teaches, because Thou hast revealed them, Who can neither deceive nor be deceived.

Act of Hope

O my God, relying on Thy almighty power and infinite mercy and promises, I hope to obtain pardon for my sins, the help of Thy grace, and life everlasting, through the merits of Jesus Christ, my Lord and Redeemer.

Act of Love

O my God, I love Thee above all things, with my whole heart and soul, because Thou art all-good and worthy of all love. I love my neighbor as myself for love of Thee. I forgive all who have injured me and ask pardon of all whom I have injured.

Guardian Angel prayer

Angel of God, my guardian dear, to whom God's love commits me here; ever this day be at my side: to light, to guard, to rule, to guide. Amen.

Anima Christi

Soul of Christ, sanctify me. Body of Christ, heal me. Blood of Christ, fill me. Water from the side of Christ, wash me. Passion of Christ, strengthen me. Good Jesus, hear me. In Thy wounds, hide me. To be separated from Thee, never permit me. From the evil enemy, defend me. At the hour of my death, call me. And bid me to come to Thee; that with Thy saints I may praise Thee, for ever and ever. Amen.

Apostles' Creed

I believe in God, the Father almighty, creator of heaven and earth. I believe in Jesus Christ, His only Son, our Lord. He was conceived by the power of the Holy Spirit and born of the Virgin Mary. He suffered under Pontius Pilate, was crucified, died, and was buried. He descended into hell. On the third day He rose again. He ascended into heaven and is seated at the right hand of the Father. He will come again to judge the living and the dead. I believe in the Holy Spirit, the holy catholic Church, the communion of saints, the forgiveness of sins, the resurrection of the body, and the life everlasting. Amen.[21]

Our Father

Our Father, who art in heaven, hollowed be Thy name. Thy kingdom come. Thy will be done on earth, as it is in heaven. Give us this day our daily bread, and forgive us our trespasses, as we forgive those who trespass against us, and lead us not into temptation, but deliver us from evil. Amen.

Hail Mary

Hail, Mary, full of grace, the Lord is with thee. Blessed art thou among women, and blessed is the fruit of thy womb, Jesus. Holy Mary, mother of God, pray for us sinners, now and at the hour of our death. Amen.

Memorare

Remember, O most gracious Virgin Mary, that never was it known that anyone who fled to thy protection, implored thy help, or sought thy intercession was left unaided. Inspired by this confidence, I fly unto thee, O Virgin of virgins, my Mother. To thee I come, before thee I stand, sinful and sorrowful. O Mother of the Word Incarnate, despise not my petitions, but in thy mercy hear and answer me. Amen.

Prayer for Vocations

Lord Jesus Christ, shepherd of souls, Who called the apostles to be fishers of men, raise up new apostles in Your holy Church. Teach them that to serve You is to reign: to possess You is to possess all things. Kindle in the hearts of our young people the fire of zeal for souls. Make them eager to spread Your Kingdom upon earth. Grant them the courage to follow You, who are the Way, the Truth, and the Life; Who live and reign for ever and ever. Amen.[22]

One of the best collections is *Handbook of Prayers*, Reverend James Socías, General editor (Princeton, NJ: Scepter Publishers, 1997), from which certain of these prayers were taken. The Glory Be, the Litany of the Sacred Heart and the Litany of the Blessed Virgin can also be found here.

[21] *CCC*, page 49–50.
[22] *Handbook of Prayers*, 62.

#BA–1 $5.95

BEGINNING APOLOGETICS 1:
How to Explain &
Defend the Catholic Faith
Father Frank Chacon & Jim Burnham

Gives clear, biblical answers to the most common objections Catholics get about their faith. *40 pages. (Spanish, #AE-1)*

#CD–1 $22.95

DEFENDING THE CATHOLIC FAITH
Jim Burnham

Shows you how to become an effective apologist, defend the Real Presence and the Church's incorruptibility, and discover the early Church Fathers. *4 talks, 3-CDs.*

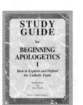

#BA1–SG $4.95

STUDY GUIDE
for Beginning Apologetics 1
Jim Burnham & Steve Wood

Guides the individual or group through 12 easy lessons. Provides discussion questions and extra material from the Bible, Catechism, and early Church Fathers. *16 pages. (#AE1-GE)*

BEGINNING APOLOGETICS 2:
How to Answer Jehovah's
Witnesses & Mormons
Father Frank Chacon & Jim Burnham

Targets these groups' major beliefs, and shows you how to refute them using Scripture, history, and common sense. *40 pages. (#AE-2)*

#BA–2 $5.95

BEGINNING APOLOGETICS 2.5
Yes! You Should Believe in the Trinity:
How to Answer Jehovah's Witnesses
Father Frank Chacon & Jim Burnham

Refutes the JWs' attack on the Trinity and provides a clear, concise theology of the Trinity. *24 pages. (#AE-2.5)*

#BA–2.5 $4.95

#BA–3 $5.95

BEGINNING APOLOGETICS 3:
How to Explain & Defend the Real
Presence of Christ in the Eucharist
Father Frank Chacon & Jim Burnham

Proves the Real Presence using Scripture, early Church Fathers, and history. Gives practical ways to increase your knowledge of the Eucharist. *40 pages.*

#BA–4 $5.95

BEGINNING APOLOGETICS 4:
How to Answer Atheists & New Agers
Father Frank Chacon & Jim Burnham

Traces the roots of atheism and New Age movement. Refutes their beliefs using sound philosophy and common sense. *40 pages.*

#BA–5 $5.95

BEGINNING APOLOGETICS 5:
How to Answer Tough
Moral Questions
Father Frank Chacon & Jim Burnham

Answers questions about abortion, contraception, euthanasia, cloning, and sexual ethics, using clear moral principles and the authoritative teachings of the Church. *40 pages.*

#BA–6 $5.95

BEGINNING APOLOGETICS 6:
How to Explain and Defend Mary
Father Frank Chacon & Jim Burnham

Answers the most common questions about Mary. Demonstrates the biblical basis for our Marian beliefs and devotions. *40 pages.*

#BA–7 $5.95

BEGINNING APOLOGETICS 7:
How to Read the Bible—A Catholic
Introduction to Interpreting &
Defending Sacred Scripture
Father Frank Chacon & Jim Burnham

Provides the basic tools to read and interpret the Bible correctly. Shows how to effectively refute the errors of some modern biblical scholars. *40 pages.*

#BA–8 $5.95

BEGINNING APOLOGETICS 8:
The End Times
Father Frank Chacon & Jim Burnham

Explains what Catholics believe about the Second Coming, the Rapture, Heaven, Hell, Purgatory, and Indulgences. Refutes the errors of the "Left Behind" rapture crowd. *40 pages.*

#AVF $2.95

THE CATHOLIC VERSE-FINDER
Jim Burnham

Organizes over 500 verses showing the biblical basis for more than 50 Catholic doctrines— *all on one sheet of paper!* This amazing "Bible cheat sheet" helps you answer the majority of non-Catholic objections. Fold it in half, put in your Bible and never be unprepared to discuss your faith again. *1 sheet laminated, printed both sides.*

BEGINNING APOLOGETICS: BEGINNER'S DELUXE KIT
Father Frank Chacon, Jim Burnham and Steve Wood have teamed up to bring you this kit. You get …

- *Beginning Apologetics 1: How to Explain and Defend the Catholic Faith*
- Companion Study Guide
- Catholic Verse-Finder
- 12-session, CD set

The whole set for one price! $44.95

All items in the kit are available separately.